REAL WORLD ECONOMICS™

How
Business
Decisions
Are Made

Mary-Lane Kamberg

ROSEN
PUBLISHING®
New York

For Roo

Published in 2012 by The Rosen Publishing Group, Inc.
29 East 21st Street, New York, NY 10010

Copyright © 2012 by The Rosen Publishing Group, Inc.

First Edition

Library of Congress Cataloging-in-Publication Data

Kamberg, Mary-Lane, 1948–
How business decisions are made/Mary-Lane Kamberg.—1st ed.
     p. cm.—(Real world economics)
Includes bibliographical references and index.
ISBN 978-1-4488-5565-0 (library binding)
1. Decision making. I. Title.
HD30.23.K266 2012
658.4'03—dc23

2011017427

Manufactured in China

CPSIA Compliance Information: Batch #W12YA: For further information, contact Rosen Publishing, New York, New York, at
1-800-237-9932.

Contents

INTRODUCTION

Have you ever opened a package that was packed with Bubble Wrap? Perhaps you've even popped the air bubbles for fun!

Bubble Wrap is a packing material with air bubbles sealed in plastic. Sealed Air manufactures and sells the product. The company began in the early 1960s. It sold wallpaper with texture. The texture came from trapped air. Wallpaper sales were too low, so the company found a new use for the idea and created Bubble Wrap as a packaging material. It kept shipments safer during shipment than current packaging products. At the time, manufacturers used cardboard boxes and wads of paper to ship items.

Dermot Dunphy changed all that; he was the chief executive officer (CEO) of Sealed Air from 1971 to 2000. When Dunphy took over as CEO, he changed the company's goal. It would not sell "packaging"; it would sell "protection." Technology set Sealed Air apart. Dunphy looked for new products that no

4

one else offered and invested in research. He hired engineers and chemists who designed packages specifically for items that Sealed Air's customers wanted to ship.

Over the years, Sealed Air has had many chances to buy another packaging company, which some people thought made sense. It could get new customers for BubbleWrap, and then its sales force could sell boxes from the newly purchased company to the same customer. However, Dunphy always said no. The purchase did not fit with the company vision. Sealed Air would lose its advantage.

Not all business decisions are that easy. And they're not all made by the CEO. At different times, employees at all levels make them. That's why managers and other workers need guidelines to help them make the best choices. Situations and choices vary, as do the roles of emotion, experience, and intuition. The process itself depends on the type of decision and who makes it.

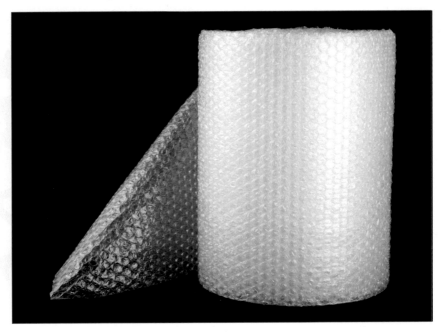

The CEO at Sealed Air, the manufacturer of Bubble Wrap, made a strategic decision to sell the packing material as "protection," not simply "packaging material."

The global economy also affects how business leaders make decisions. The fast pace of international business requires good business judgment. It also depends on up-to-the-minute information. The process of making decisions often differs from culture to culture, so business leaders must be able to use more than one decision-making method.

Many business decisions work out for the best. But what happens when they don't? The decision process can be simple or complicated. Based on logic or intuition. Or both.

So how are business decisions made?

CHAPTER ONE
HOW ARE GOOD DECISIONS MADE?

Life is full of decisions. You may have already made several of your own today. What should you wear? Do you need extra help with your math homework? Should you go to the mall with your friends? Or play basketball in the driveway with your brother? Some decisions are easy to make; some are as simple as choosing a sock color. But others result from a set of steps that you may not even know you follow.

Like you, business leaders make decisions every day, and their decisions affect their companies' profits. Profit is the amount of money left after subtracting the costs of doing business. The decisions can also affect the employees, competitors, customers, and others.

When faced with a question or problem, a business leader first defines the goal. What does he or she want? For example, suppose a company leader needs to choose how to ship a product to a customer. Is it more important to find the method that

Some business decisions are made by company leaders. Others are made by teams assigned to the role. The teams often consist of department managers or other employees.

costs the least? Or is it more important to find the one that gets the product delivered on time? If the company offers free shipping, the cheapest way would be best. It would cost the company less money. But if the company is shipping a keyboard

for a rock concert, the best method is the one that gets the instrument to the arena on time.

Once the question is clear, the leader determines which decision-making process he or she will use. An executive may make the decision on his or her own. At other times, a team of department managers and other employees may participate. At this point, decision makers need information—lots of it. The information they need often includes the company's financial reports. But information from outside the company is also important. What is the economy like? What are competitors doing? Will customers like the change? What obstacles might we face?

The next step is to create a list of choices. A group of managers and other employees can use brainstorming techniques to come up with the list. But the executive must be sure that participants feel comfortable expressing their thoughts. One way to come up with ideas is to look for a way to achieve a result that is the opposite of the goal. Suppose the goal is to get more teenage customers. The decision team might discuss ways to keep teens away. This new way of looking at the problem boosts creativity. Another way to come up with ideas is to search the Web for ways other businesses have achieved the same or a similar goal.

Once the list is made, each choice must be weighed. Decision makers look for the pros (positives) and cons (negatives) of each choice. They consider the element of risk in each, and they compare risk to possible gain. They also look at whether the company has the necessary time and money for the choice. Finally, do personnel have the required skills and experience to put the idea into action?

Sometimes there are many good choices. The task is to determine which is best for the goal and the situation. Once the choice is made, the process is not over, however.

PUTTING DECISIONS TO WORK

The next step is to announce the decision and put it in place. CEOs and managers should follow these steps:

Step 1. Help employees understand the process used to reach the decision. Let them see that careful thought went into it.

Step 2. Be honest about the facts used to evaluate the choices. Talk about the cause and size of the problem. Explain what could happen if it isn't solved. Or explain the opportunity. The more information you share, the fewer rumors and criticism will result.

Step 3. Help employees put the decision in place. Give them a clear set of directions. Include goals that can be measured. Discuss some obstacles they may face.

The Head or the Heart?

Here are three opinions on whether decisions are better made by the head or the heart:

- **Plato, the ancient Greek philosopher (428–348 BCE), let experience enter the process. He said, "A good decision is based on knowledge, not on numbers."**

- **Alden M. Hayashi, a senior editor at the *Harvard Business Review*, said that intuition may be useful in making decisions, but only along with reason.**

- **Kim Wallace, chairman of the marketing research firm Wallace and Washburn, once told the *Harvard Business Review*, "The key to making a decision is to delay the decision until it makes logical sense and it feels right. The two sides of the brain must agree."**

Once the decision is put into action, leaders must observe the results. A decision is only as good as how well it works. If the outcome is bad, they must seek answers to what went wrong. They should try to learn all they can about how the decision was made. And they should look for ways they can improve the process for future choices. Leaders should also review good results. The experience will help them with future decisions.

What Are the Ingredients of Good Decisions?

- Good decisions are based on good information. One place to get it from is the company's financial records. Accounting is the function of keeping track of the financial activities of a business. What does it cost to make the product? How do the current year's sales compare to last year's? How many repeat customers are there? Knowing how to understand and interpret this information is an important decision-making skill.

- Good decisions are sometimes based on expert advice. Some experts already work for the company; others work outside of it. If someone is considering purchasing an office supply company, for instance, he or she should consult people in the office supply industry. This is especially important if the leader has little experience in that area.

- Good decisions rely on the decision maker's ability to keep an open mind. It's human nature to favor the first information received. What seems like the best choice at first may not turn out to be. The decision maker must be willing to change his or her mind after considering all the choices.

- Good decisions depend on the natural ability of the people involved in the process. Some leaders

Good decisions depend on good information. A business leader must be able to understand and interpret the company's financial records, as well as information from outside the company.

just have a knack for spotting a good thing. For example, two graduate students showed their new search engine to one of the founders of Sun Microsystems. He invested money and made a nice profit. Today, the search engine is known as Google.

- Good decisions sometimes result from the experience of the person making them. Leaders learn from every decision they make—no matter how it turns out. The more practice making decisions, the better.

What Role Does Emotion Play?

Business leaders use facts and logic to make decisions. But what role does emotion play? Have you ever thought about making a choice that just didn't "feel" right? Human beings use logic and reason to understand and get along in the world. But emotion is also at work.

Call it intuition, business instinct, or gut reaction: decision makers often rely on it to make choices. In fact, IBM's general manager John Granger says that 75 percent of business leaders trust their feelings and experience more than analysis of information. This human factor is often an important part of the decision-making process. The fact is that humans tend to react emotionally to a situation before they react with logic. And many people believe that their first idea is the best. In a business situation, leaders must listen to their hearts as well as their minds.

The human factor is an important part of decision making. Facts and logic often give way to emotion, experience, and intuition. Most experts agree that both logic and emotion work together.

RESTRICTIONS ON DECISION MAKING

In a perfect world, decisions would be easy. People could list choices and pick the best one. However, in the more complicated world of business, some options just won't work. For example, a state-of-the-art piece of machinery might make production easier, but it may cost too much.

A business's own policy may get in the way of one of the possible choices. A company may be dedicated to using "green" products, which protect the environment. So the person who orders paper won't be able to take advantage of a sale on paper made without recycled content.

15

Sometimes the human element keeps a business leader from choosing a particular plan of action. Unhappy employees might resist management's efforts to act on an unpopular decision. The human element can also include employees who lack the skills to support a decision. For instance, new computer software might improve business activities, but what if employees don't know how to use it? The cost of training or the hassle of hiring a new employee could make the option a bad choice. Lack of necessary hardware to support the software may also keep a decision maker from buying it.

Other restrictions on choices are laws and regulations. A restaurant owner might want to create a dining area where people can smoke. However, if the city has a law against smoking in restaurants, the owner cannot make that choice.

MYTHS and FACTS

MYTH Business decisions are rational.

FACT Decisions often involve emotion, self-interest, or impulsive or irrational factors. Even a rational decision process has flaws, especially if a leader is looking for the "one" right answer—which may or may not exist.

MYTH It's best to wait until all the facts are in and alternatives evaluated before making a decision.

FACT Sometimes delaying a decision becomes a decision not to act at all. Opportunity may be lost.

MYTH Making a final decision is the end of the decision-making process.

FACT Care must be taken to put the decision in action. The decision also must be analyzed after the fact to evaluate good and bad choices and make changes in the process as needed.

CHAPTER TWO

WHY BUSINESSES NEED DECISION MAKING

Businesses exist to make money. During the course of business, leaders face a wide variety of choices. The choices may help the business cut costs or increase profits—or both.

Business leaders must make decisions when faced with questions, problems, and opportunities, such as:

- What is our overall plan?
- What products or services shall we make?
- What price will we charge?
- What shall we pay employees?
- Which health care plan shall we offer?
- Which company shall we use for deliveries?
- Where will we buy the materials we need?
- Shall we buy the building down the street?
- Should we buy another business?

Business decisions fall into three groups: strategy, tactics, and operations. Let's take a look at each of them.

Strategy, Tactics, and Operations

Here's how the different types of decisions fit into a business. Company executives choose the company's strategy. For example, do we want to offer our customers "low cost" or "exceptional customer service"? They decide to offer exceptional service. Managers then choose the tactics. How will they put the strategy into place? Perhaps they'll create a program to train employees on how to greet customers. Or they may create a guide for handling customer complaints. With the strategy and tactics clear, employees are able to make day-to-day operational decisions that line up with the company's goals.

STRATEGIC DECISIONS

Strategy is the overall plan for a business. At Sealed Air (the Bubble Wrap company discussed in this book's introduction), for example, the company strategy is to use technology to set itself apart from competitors.

Strategy determines the long-term direction for a company. It covers as many as five to fifteen years into the future. One example is a decision to open forty-five new stores over the next six years.

Strategic decisions also tend to be those with the most risk. These include such questions as whether to purchase major pieces of machinery or buy another company. Decision makers must guess whether the machinery will be worth its price. Will it pay for itself by saving time? Or will it improve the quality

The strategy that will guide a company over the next five to ten years is determined by its top leaders. Managers make the tactical decisions that put the strategy in place.

of the finished product? If one company purchases another, the new one can add profits, but there also is the risk of losses. Strategic decisions affect a company's profits. They also affect whether a business survives at all. (Remember, businesses are

20

in business to make money. If they fail to make money—or lose money—they may have to go out of business.)

Owners, boards of directors, CEOs, and top managers have the responsibility for making strategic decisions.

TACTICAL DECISIONS

Tactics are the plans a company uses to put the strategy in place. These decisions affect business over several months or years. Examples include what kind of advertising program to use and how many employees to hire.

Strategic decisions stay in place for a long time, while tactical ones are often reviewed and changed. Managers are in charge of tactics—they make these kinds of decisions.

Suppose a car dealership sets a sales goal of 720 used cars in a year. Managers set a goal of making at least $2,000 on each car. However, after six months, only 275 cars have sold. The company is halfway through the year. But sales have not reached one-half the goal (720 divided by 2 equals 360). The dealer is 85 cars short. Customers who thought the price was too high went to other dealers to buy their cars.

Managers may decide to change their tactics. Perhaps they'll lower the amount they make per car to $1,250. Customers will

A car dealership's management team may adjust tactics to meet its annual sales goal. While strategic decisions stay in place for five to ten years, tactical decisions are often reevaluated as necessary.

get better deals. The dealer will sell more cars. This plan may increase sales enough to reach the goal.

OPERATIONAL DECISIONS

Tactics guide a company's daily activities. Operational decisions cover the details. Operational decisions are also called administrative decisions. These are the details of the overall plan. Like tactics, operations always fit into the company's strategy.

One example is choosing a new delivery service. Another might be how to handle merchandise returns. Operational decisions guide all employees as they make decisions during the day.

Will Machines Make Decisions?

The U.S. military has brought battlefield robots to life. Once seen only in science fiction movies, robots have been in use since 2003 in wars in Iraq and Afghanistan. According to the Public Broadcasting Service (PBS), the military has more than six thousand of them. For instance, the TALON robot deals with explosive devices. The robots save lives of American soldiers by doing dangerous jobs.

Now there are robots with guns. One is called MAARS, for Modular Advanced Armed Robotic System. It carries a light machine gun. The military could use it to patrol an area or fight an enemy. It hasn't been used yet, but an early version called SWORDS was tested in Iraq. These robots are under a soldier's control. The decision to fire the gun belongs to a human.

However, in the future, robots may be able to identify the enemy, choose targets, and fire. These robots do not exist yet. However, technology may advance to the point where the human element disappears from some decision-making.

DECISIONS WORKING TOGETHER

Strategic, tactical, and operational decisions must be in tune with each other. If the business strategy is to give good service, but the CEO praises each manager who keeps department costs low, employees won't know what to do. Will they try to make customers happy, or try to save money?

Executives should also be sure that the method used to determine employees' pay reflects the company strategy. For

23

All of a company's decisions should support its overall goals. If the tactics and operational decisions fail to match the company's strategies, managers and employees will fail to achieve the targets.

example, a company might choose the customer service strategy. But a department manager might earn a bonus for saving money. When faced with a customer complaint, the manager is more likely to choose the action that saves the company money instead of the one that gives the best customer service. (He'll get a higher bonus.) The company's decision-making process will soon fail to match its strategy.

A Publisher Makes Decisions

Whispering Prairie Press publishes a magazine called *Kansas City Voices*. The magazine features poems, stories, and artwork. The board of directors determined the strategy: to produce a magazine of top-quality art and writing.

Some tactical decisions included:

- How will we let artists and writers know about the magazine? (Managers decided to advertise in a national magazine for poets and writers. They also contacted art galleries to ask artists to submit their work.)
- How will we pay for our costs? (They decided to sell advertising and subscriptions. They also asked for donations from people who support the arts.)
- How will we select what goes into each issue? (They decided to find two editors each for prose, poetry, and art.)

Some operational decisions included:

- What type of paper shall we use? (The production manager decided to use expensive, quality paper. A cheaper choice let the color ink on the artwork show through on the other side of the page. The decision followed the strategy of producing a quality magazine. The expensive paper showed off the artwork at its best.)
- Which word processing software program should we use? (The editors chose the word processing software that most professional writers prefer. That made it easier to get the best writers.)

WHO DECIDES WHAT?

The right people at the right levels should make business decisions. The right people and levels vary based on the question. Company leaders must assign certain people to make certain decisions. Suppose the business wants to add a product to its line. What will the features be? Who will decide? Should it be the manufacturing people who design it? Or the marketing people who will sell it? Or should the teams work together?

Another consideration is where a decision is to be made. Some decisions are best made at the top level, or headquarters of the company. Others are best left to local offices. In general, major purchases for a company occur at the headquarters level. So do decisions that involve some cheaper items that the company buys a lot of. The company can make a deal for a lower price.

For example, a large corporation orders three thousand new desks for all of its branch offices. It asks a furniture manufacturer for a quantity discount. Instead of paying $250 for each desk, the company only pays $175 each. If the local branch orders only one desk, it would not have to pay the higher price. The manufacturer makes less per desk. But because it sells so many desks, it makes more money. The corporation saves money on the purchase. And the local office gets its desk for less.

In other situations, the local office may be the best place to make decisions. A manager at a branch office may be able to make a better deal on oil changes for company cars than an executive at a faraway headquarters. The manager lives in the area and knows which mechanics have the best reputation. He or she can also take advantage of local specials and coupons. The manager is in a better position to make the choice than someone out of town.

CHAPTER THREE

METHODS AND TOOLS

In the business world, decisions are more than choices. They require looking at the likely good and bad results of each choice. The goal is to find the choice with the best effect on the company—or the one with the fewest bad effects. Decision makers try to find the choice with the best chance of reaching the goal.

But first, they make many small decisions on the way to the main one. What is the issue? Is it a problem or an opportunity? Who will make the decision? Who will be affected by it? How will the decision be applied? The answers to these questions determine the decision-making method to be used.

Some Ways to Make Decisions

The process of making decisions takes many different forms. The first—and often least successful—is the knee-jerk reaction. A knee-jerk reaction is based on emotion. The person decides a course of action off the top of his or her head. The decision is

Should a restaurant manager fire a cook who is late on the spot? Firing the cook may be the right decision. But a better decision-making method is to gather information first.

quick, and it's based only on the first information that comes in. There is no attempt to get any more facts. And there's no time for testing alternatives.

A restaurant cook comes to work an hour late. The boss fires the cook in a fit of anger. This is an example of a knee-jerk reaction. The boss would make a better decision if he or she took the time to calm down. He may decide to fire the cook later after gathering more information. The records might show that the cook has a habit of showing up late. The decision to fire him or her may be the right one. On the other hand, what if the records show that the employee has never been late before? A knee-jerk reaction might cause the boss to lose a valuable employee. The boss could decide to give only a warning. Either way, checking the facts gives the boss a better chance of arriving at a good decision.

MAJORITY RULE

Another way to make a decision is majority rule. Take a vote. See which option wins. This method works well for employees who are choosing a theme for the annual holiday party. However, few business leaders take a vote on issues that affect the life of the company. Most businesses share financial records and other information only with top executives and managers.

Still, some companies share that data with all employees. They use a plan called open-book management. Officials let employees see the company's financial records. The employees don't vote on decisions. However, the company includes all employees in the decision process.

Zingerman's Community of Businesses in Ann Arbor, Michigan, uses this method. Zingerman's businesses are

At Zingerman's Delicatessen in Ann Arbor, Michigan, management gives employees access to the company's financial records. Individuals track various parts of the business, and everyone participates in the decision-making process.

specialty food stores. The first was Zingerman's Delicatessen. Each business has its own food specialty. The owners let all employees see the financial records. And all employees share decision-making duties.

A different individual monitors each part of the business. He or she posts the information collected. All employees can see the numbers for sales, expenses, debts, payroll, and other information. They discuss the information at weekly meetings. Employees can see the costs of running the business. They also see how their work affects profits and look for ways to cut costs. They also look for better ways to do their jobs, and they understand why owners and managers make the decisions they do.

WEIGHING THE PROS AND CONS

Another way to make a decision is to make two lists, one for each possible action. Draw a vertical line on a piece of paper. On one side of the line, list all the advantages of the choice. On the other, list the disadvantages. Use a separate piece of paper for each option.

Not every item on the lists needs to carry the same weight. Say you're looking for office space. You might like the layout of one of the choices, but the location of another may be better. Or the price of a third may be the lowest. Compare all the options and look for the choices with the most good points. Choose that one.

What if two or more choices seem equally positive? In that case, focus on the bad points, and choose the alternative with the fewest negatives.

WORKING TOGETHER

Some business decisions result from an effort to build agreement among those who are making the decision. This agreement is called consensus. Consensus is not necessarily total agreement. Instead, it is a general agreement. In other words, most team members can accept it. And few oppose it altogether.

To build consensus, business leaders try to get everyone involved and listen to others' opinions without judging them. When a team reaches consensus, each person who participated in the discussion is more likely to accept the decision.

One way to build consensus is to hold one or more meetings before the final meeting where the decision is announced.

31

At the "before" meetings, decisions are introduced to a person or small group first, giving the person or group a chance to discuss the idea. The business leader can address any objections. The smaller meetings help the leader gain agreement before taking the issue to a larger audience. That leader creates a base of support one or two important people at a time. When the leader announces the decision, no one says anything against it. Any disagreements have already been addressed.

TECH TOOLS

In order to make good decisions, today's business leaders need information. They need it fast, and they need to act fast on it. However, many say they aren't getting it. In a recent IBM survey of 225 business leaders, 50 percent said they don't have enough information to do their jobs. More than 33 percent said they have trouble getting information that matters. And they can't use the information they do get to make forecasts or evaluate risk.

In the past, bookkeepers kept track of business activities by hand. They used new tools as they became available; adding machines followed by calculators helped them perform the mathematics. Financial reports went to business leaders to interpret and act on. About twenty-five years ago, spreadsheets and simple accounting software for personal computers helped track information, but the numbers that appeared on those reports reflected only past activities.

Today, information technology, or IT, provides better information—sometimes in real time. Real time means a computer function happens "live," in an instant.

Adding machines once helped businesses track activities. Today, new technology interprets data as well as records it. Business intelligence software also lets business leaders predict outcomes of various choices before putting them in place.

For example, a warehouse manager using a real-time system can track every product, both as it comes into the warehouse and as it's shipped out. IT uses advanced mathematics and powerful hardware. It lets business leaders make decisions and take action within seconds or minutes instead of within days, weeks, or even months.

Today's technology not only collects and stores information; it interprets it, too. Electronic analysis of information for decision making is known as business intelligence, or BI. BI is a decision support system that gives decision makers the tools they need to make good choices.

How Much Business Data Is There?

The world is experiencing a global information explosion. It's hard to keep track of it all. In 2010, IBM's Granger, speaking at the IBM Summit at Start (a conference begun by the Prince of Wales to show what a more energy-efficient, cleaner, and healthier future could look like), said business data is growing by 57 percent per year. He said the amount of data worldwide would be 988 exabytes by the end of 2010. An exabyte is a unit of computer storage. One byte equals eight digits. One exabyte equals 1,152,921,504,606,846,976 bytes. Just one exabyte can store fifty thousand years' worth of DVD-quality video.

SEEING THE FUTURE

Some software can predict the future by letting leaders run "what-if" experiments to see which choices hold the most

34

promise. For example, they can run the numbers to see the effects of setting different prices. Leaders can see what will happen at each of several prices. They don't have to actually change the prices and wait to see what happens.

BI helps leaders make faster and better decisions. Recently, a business research firm called the Aberdeen Group conducted a survey. It found that companies that used BI cut the time between getting information and acting on it by an average of 8 percent over a year. The survey also found that 25 percent of the best retail companies using BI saw their profits increase 10 percent in one year.

With those kinds of improvements, many businesses are trying to use BI to gain a competitive edge. An IBM study revealed recently that 83 percent of chief information officers (CIOs) said BI is the best way to become more competitive. The Gartner research firm reports that worldwide sales of BI software were more than $9.7 billion in 2010. Gartner predicted that worldwide sales would reach more than $11.3 billion by 2012.

CHAPTER FOUR
DECISIONS IN THE GLOBAL ECONOMY

In 2010, the Safety Research and Strategies research firm found 2,274 cases of Toyota cars speeding up on their own. The firm also found reports of 275 car accidents from this problem over the previous ten years. The National Highway Traffic Safety Administration (NHTSA) said that fifty-two people died in those accidents.

Toyota had learned some of this information over the past decade. However, the Japanese automaker waited until 2009 to recall millions of Camrys and Corollas. (A recall is an action by a product's manufacturer.) The company asked people who bought the cars to return them for repair. Additional recalls of Toyota models followed in 2010 and 2011.

The Associated Press reported in 2010 that many Toyota owners sued the company. They said the safety recalls caused the value of their cars to drop. They claimed that Toyota knew about the safety problems but didn't tell buyers about them. The press reported that eighty-nine class-action lawsuits had

In 2010, Toyota recalled more than two million vehicles to fix problems with the accelerator pedal. By American standards, the Japanese automaker was slow to address the problem due to cultural differences in decision making.

been filed. Before 2011, a class-action lawsuit was one in which people with similar cases join forces. Under federal law at the time, a class-action suit needed more than one hundred people who asked for more than $5 million.

Those lawsuits weren't the only ones filed against Toyota. People who owned stock in the company also sued for financial losses. Still others sued for injuries or deaths.

Many said that Toyota waited too long to do anything about the problem. The business decision that caused the long waiting period may have been based in Japanese culture. For one thing, lawsuits in Japan are far less common than in the United States. The decision makers may not have realized the effect of the delay. Also, Japanese society has greater respect for rank and authority than American society does. Workers in Japan are less likely to challenge a boss than workers in the United States.

But perhaps most important is the idea of saving face. People in Eastern cultures value a good self-image. They don't want to admit a mistake. The embarrassment of looking bad in the eyes of others is strong. Businesspeople from Eastern countries may even continue a conflict to avoid a blow to their image.

Decision makers for international businesses must consider the ways people from different countries use the decision-making process. The decision makers may face challenges based on cultural differences. At the same time, it is important not to lump all people from the same country together. No one can predict an individual's attitude or behavior. There are always great differences within each culture. However, international business leaders must be sensitive to values and communication styles that differ from their own.

CULTURAL DIFFERENCES

As in the Toyota example, a cultural attitude toward authority affects decision making in international business. In some societies, workers get different treatment based on their place in the organization. In other countries, leaders and workers have more of an "everybody's equal" attitude. People from the two cultures may clash when it comes to making choices.

For instance, American managers were discussing a business decision with managers from the same company in Korea.

There's Hertz and There's "Not Exactly"

The car rental company Hertz uses BI to increase customer satisfaction scores. After each rental, the company asks customers about their experiences: Was the car clean? How did it run? How did employees treat you?

In the past, Hertz used paper surveys, telephone calls, and comments posted on its Web site to get the answers. It could take as much as three weeks to get the data. If a customer had a bad experience, weeks passed before managers learned about it.

Using BI technology, Hertz now gets customer reactions every day. Comments come in from smartphones and other wireless devices. If a customer has a bad experience, the local manager can make it right within twenty-four hours. Thanks to BI, Hertz's customer satisfaction scores rose every month in 2010 over the same period in 2009, according to *CIO Insight* magazine.

The Americans thought things were going too slowly. They complained to the Koreans' supervisor. Korean culture values respect based on a person's rank. When the Americans complained to someone of higher authority, they embarrassed the Koreans. The Americans failed to show proper respect to their Korean counterparts. The Americans could not solve the conflict. Their bosses in the United States had to go to Korea to show respect at the proper level.

In many cases, decision making in Western cultures differs from that in the East. In Western nations, the goal is to find

Cultural differences affect the way leaders in international businesses make decisions. Leaders must be sensitive to values and communication styles that differ from the ones in their home country.

the answer to a question or a problem. In the East, however, the goal is to come to agreement. The focus is on defining the question. Discussions even include whether a decision needs to be made at all.

FAST OR SLOW?

Cultures also differ on how fast decisions should be made. They also differ about how much data they need to gather and interpret. American managers, for instance, tend to decide faster with less information than managers in other countries.

In one case reported in the *Harvard Business Review*, a Brazilian manager for an American company tried to buy products from a Korean company for the South American office. On the first day of discussions, the Brazilian and American representatives agreed with the Koreans on three points.

The next day, the Brazilian and Americans thought they would start talking about the fourth point. However, the Koreans wanted to go back over the first three points again. Their goal was harmony. The Americans thought the Koreans meant they agreed when they said, "Yes." However, the Koreans meant, "I'm listening. I understand you." They did not mean that they agreed.

What a society values shows up in odd ways. For instance Mexican culture values humility. In order to point out a problem, a Mexican worker is likely to ask questions about it. To do otherwise would seem like bragging. Americans might misunderstand the Mexican's style. They might think the Mexican doesn't know what he or she is talking about because he or she keeps asking questions.

The Role of Social Media in Business Decisions

Business leaders around the world use social media as a tool for making decisions. A survey by Research and Markets reported in 2010 found that CEOs, directors, and managers of international companies use social networks for business.

The survey of 356 professionals from 25 countries was conducted online. The companies they worked for ranged in size from one hundred full-time employees to fifty thousand. The study found that business leaders belong to many different social networks, particularly LinkedIn, Facebook, and Twitter. It also found that business leaders have high levels of trust in the information they get through these contacts. The main uses of social networks are to connect with other professionals and work together to solve problems or make other decisions.

COMMUNICATION STYLES

Leaders from Western cultures often use a direct style to communicate. What they say is what they mean. However, businesspeople from Eastern cultures may only hint at different levels of meaning. In general, those from Eastern countries can understand the Western approach. However, those from the West often have trouble figuring out what those from Eastern countries are trying to say.

English is the language of international business. However, nonnative English speakers sometimes have trouble showing their knowledge. They may speak with an accent or have a limited English vocabulary. Native English speakers

Suspense author Brad Meltzer (also the host of the television show *Decoded*) used networking via e-mail to determine the title of his novel *The Book of Lies*.

may incorrectly think the workers aren't smart enough to do their work.

Communication style also includes the way someone says things. For example, some American engineers working in Ireland with Israelis from the same company had to make a decision. The team discussed the choices. At first, the Americans thought the Israelis were being too forceful. They seemed too pushy when stating their opinions. However, the Americans soon noticed the Israelis treated each other the same way. The Americans grew to accept the way the Israelis joined the discussions.

The Effects of the World Wide Web

According to Research and Markets, a market research company, more than one billion people worldwide are connected to the Internet. Four billion people use mobile phones. In any one week, as many as four hundred million people exchange information online. These technologies affect decision making in international business. They contribute to a worldwide virtual work environment and make it easy to consult others. They can reach experts anywhere in the world in seconds and instantly share information that once took weeks or months to get.

Many businesses use social networks to communicate with customers. Many have a Web presence on Facebook, LinkedIn, or Twitter. Some even use social networks as decision-making tools. A manufacturer can hold virtual meetings with customers anywhere in the world to get their opinions. BI lets them measure and analyze the responses.

When novelist Brad Meltzer needed a title for his latest novel, he asked his fans. Should the book be called *The Book of Truth* or *The Book of Lies*? In a group message, Meltzer e-mailed fans who had contacted him through his Web site. He compared the responses and made a decision. *The Book of Lies* was released by Grand Central Publishing in 2008.

CHAPTER FIVE
WHEN THINGS GO WRONG

In the early 1990s, the Nike athletic shoe and clothing company signed contracts with factories in Indonesia, Vietnam, and China. Like other multinational businesses, Nike was attracted to the low wages it could pay overseas workers. In April 1997, Nike factory workers in Indonesia went on strike (work stoppage) to protest low pay.

Nike workers in Vietnam also went on strike over wages, and then Chinese workers joined the strikers. The Chinese added dangerous working conditions to their complaints. Other companies also paid low wages in those countries, but human rights groups put pressure on Nike. As a result, the company got a lot of bad publicity.

Nike's earlier decisions about which factories to use, how much to pay workers, and which materials to use had gone terribly wrong. The company's executives did not like the bad publicity. They made decisions to improve working conditions. They increased pay rates for workers. They also replaced harmful petroleum-based chemicals with less dangerous ones.

NIKE
EASY GOING
IRRESPONSIBLE

NIKE
WHERE IS YOUR
COMMITMENT

NIKE
EASY GOING
RESPONSIBLE

NIKE
WHERE IS YOUR
COMMITMENT

NIKE
WHERE IS YOUR
COMMITMENT

NIKE
TERORIS

When business decisions go wrong, a company may get negative publicity that damages its reputation in the global marketplace. Nike decided to pay low wages overseas, but factory workers protested.

Critics continued to complain about Nike's practices, so in 2002 the company issued new safety and working condition rules for its factories. Nike created a team to monitor the new rules. It also allowed independent inspectors to check on the factories.

Not every business decision turns out to be a good one. It's important to review decisions after they're made to see how they are working out. IBM's Granger says 42 percent of business leaders think they have made bad decisions.

So what goes wrong? And how can businesses keep bad decisions to a minimum?

Types of Self-Interest

Self-interest should not get in the way of a good business decision. Here are some ways a decision maker could put his or her interests ahead of the company's:

- A desire to look good to the boss.
- A desire to be popular among other employees.
- A desire to enjoy a better lifestyle. (A leader might choose the option that lets him or her spend more time with family.)
- A desire to make more money for himself or herself.
- A desire to have fun at work. The decision maker might make a choice that lets him or her do preferred tasks. Jobs he or she doesn't like go to others—who may not have the skills needed to complete the tasks.

Experts agree that the worst business decisions are ones that are never made. A business leader may delay a choice to gather more information. Or he or she may worry about making the wrong move. No decision is a decision. If nothing is decided, nothing changes. Lack of action may have bad results for the company.

WHERE TO LOOK FOR ANSWERS

When things go wrong, it's important to learn why. That way, future decisions will have a better chance for success. Sometimes the decision was right, but it was not put into action correctly. If workers don't think a decision was right, they might not follow it. So the first question to ask is, "Was the decision explained and put into action?" If not, the leader must take steps to correct the situation.

If the decision was put to work correctly, the leader must look elsewhere. (Of course, leaders should also analyze good decisions to learn what went right.) In bad decisions, something got in the way of the decision process. Maybe the goal of the decision was wrong, or it wasn't identified. Perhaps the decision maker overlooked a major risk, or the market changed. A change in the business environment could make a decision go wrong.

When analyzing the decision-making process, leaders should include such questions as:

- What did we expect?
- Why did we think that?
- Why didn't those things happen?
- What can we learn from the failure?

Leaders should apply what they learn to future decisions. Perhaps they should change the decision-making method used. Or perhaps they should assign a different person or team to make similar decisions. Leaders who learn from a bad decision have a better chance of making better decisions in the future.

Decision-Making Obstacles

Anyone can make a mistake. But bad business decisions often share similarities. Here are some common ways a business leader can make a bad decision:

- **Emotions get in the way. Someone who feels strongly about something finds making a rational decision difficult.**
- **Rivalries and friendships cloud the picture. A decision maker makes decisions to help friends or hurt rivals, rather than make the business better.**
- **Past experience does not apply. A leader thinks the situation is similar to one in the past. He or she makes a similar decision. However, the new situation is different. The leader ignores the differences and makes the wrong choice.**
- **Self-interest plays a part. A decision maker decides in favor of the choice that is better for him or her, rather than what is best for the company.**
- **The leader chooses short-term goals over long-term ones. Short-term choices may pay off sooner, but they may not be best for the company over time.**
- **The leader uses the wrong decision method.**

49

Emotions sometimes get in the way of good business judgment. If someone feels strongly about something, he or she may find it difficult to make a decision that is best for the company.

The way a good decision should be made depends on the type of situation. Using the wrong method for the situation may be the cause of a bad decision. Situations can be simple, complicated, complex, or chaotic.

A simple situation is one in which all aspects of the problem and possible solutions are known. The best practice is obvious. Even a low-level employee can make the decision. For instance, if a customer wants to return a purchase, any employee can follow the company's return policy.

A complicated situation is one in which there may be more than one good answer. The business leader realizes which

Improper Connections Can Lead to Bad Decisions

A decision maker who has a strong attachment to people, places, or things may show bias toward one or more choices. Leaders should be aware of the effect of these connections on the decision-making process:

- **Favorite managers or employees.** A decision maker could lean toward a choice that benefits certain coworkers.
- **Friends from outside the work environment.** A leader could buy office supplies from his or her neighbor's business, even if the items are cheaper elsewhere.
- **Certain divisions of the company.** A decision maker who started in the sales department may decide in favor of that department, even when another choice that favors the production department would be better overall.
- **Symbols, logos, favorite products.** A leader might not want to stop producing an item that he or she likes, even though it isn't selling well.
- **Locations.** A leader who needs to choose a place for a new office or headquarters may favor cities he or she has visited or worked in.

information he or she doesn't know. The leader relies on experts to analyze the choices. For example, a company manager may consult with an auto mechanic before deciding whether to fix or replace a company truck.

A complex situation is one in which the decision maker doesn't even know what he or she needs to know. Coming up with alternatives may require experiments, such as using BI. Leaders must look for patterns among choices before they can figure out which ones will work best. For example, a business leader might ask for BI to see what effect a layoff will have on profits.

Finally, a chaotic situation is one like the Nike example at the beginning of this chapter. Things seem to go wrong all at the same time, so leaders must reestablish order before making further decisions.

What Went Wrong at General Motors?

A change in the decision-making process at General Motors (GM) may have led to the automaker's downfall. In 2008, GM asked the federal government for a bailout. A bailout is a loan for money to keep a company from going out of business. Like other manufacturers, GM had agreed to expensive contracts to cover retirement income and health care issues, but critics said that GM's decision-making processes contributed to the downfall.

GM was founded in 1908. Its first car was the Buick. The next year, the company added Oldsmobile and Cadillac. Later brands included Chevrolet and Pontiac. Each model had its own division. The division manager led all parts of the business for each brand. The manager was responsible for design, production, marketing, and sales. The system helped each model create its own identity. The brands developed strong customer loyalty. GM made good profits for its owners.

In 2008, Rick Wagoner, CEO of General Motors, accepted financial aid from the U.S. government. He predicted that the automaker would meet the profitability tests the government required as a condition of the loan.

But in the 1960s, GM leaders changed the way they made decisions. Division managers no longer ran the show. Instead, the decision-making process moved to company headquarters. For example, all GM models began to use the same parts. That may have made sense financially. Buying more of something usually makes the cost lower. But in some cases, the "shared" parts actually cost GM more money. The result was that customers had trouble telling the brands apart. By the time GM needed help from the U.S. government, its decision-making process had become too slow to respond to the car-buying public. Many former GM customers changed to other brands of cars.

CHAPTER SIX
BUSINESS DECISIONS IN REAL LIFE

‖‖‖‖‖‖‖‖‖‖‖‖‖‖‖‖‖‖‖‖‖‖‖‖‖‖‖‖‖‖‖‖‖

Businesses require decisions every day. Some may affect only a small number of employees or customers, while others can result in major changes that affect the direction the company takes in the future. Here are three examples of such real-life decisions and how they were made.

GROWING "SMALL"

Between 1990 and 2000, the Starbucks Coffee Company was a corporation on the "grow." It opened its first store in Seattle, Washington, in 1971. According to the company's timeline, it had eighty-four stores in 1990. By 2000, there were 3,501 stores in the United States and 15 foreign countries.

Starbucks is a coffee roaster and retailer. It sells coffee in café-style shops. The shops are designed to create a sense of community among the customers. A company executive wanted to create the same atmosphere he had seen in similar shops in Milan, Italy. Customers gathered in the bars in Italy to read newspapers and talk about issues of the day.

Starbucks' early marketing plan was to open stores only in major cities. The stores were close together, so a district manager could visit each one every few days. It also made it easy to deliver supplies, including fresh bakery items.

In 2000, Orin Smith took over as CEO. Critics doubted the company could grow any more. Smith disagreed. He wanted to open more stores in big cities, perhaps in such unusual locations as big office buildings and retail stores. He also wanted to open stores in small towns.

Smith visited many small towns. When he did, he said people begged him to open stores there. People who had gone to Starbucks in major metropolitan areas

In 2000, experts inside and outside the Starbucks Coffee Company focused on building new stores overseas. They thought that small towns in America could not support a Starbucks. They were wrong.

like Chicago and New York wrote letters to the company asking for stores in their towns, as did many small-town mayors. Smith believed in the idea.

However, the odds were against him. His management team said that stores spread out across a state would be too hard to manage. It would cost too much and take too much travel time. They also said getting fresh bakery products would be difficult over a large area. And they thought small-town populations could not support a store that sold expensive coffee, even if it tasted good.

The company's past experience went against the idea, too. During the 1990s, Starbucks had opened a few stores in small towns near Spokane, Washington. Sales were good, but profits were low. The cost of managing the stores was too high, and delivering supplies was hard. The staff said that, at most, only one thousand small towns in the nation could support a Starbucks store. Smith would have to forget about his plan.

Smith went about his other duties. One of those jobs was to supervise operations in other countries. Smith took a routine trip to New Zealand and visited Starbucks stores there. He saw a big difference from the company's activities in America. In New Zealand, most of the stores were in small, rural towns—and the stores were doing well. Their management teams had solved the challenges that the American analysts had presented.

First, a Starbucks store manager position was one of the best-paying jobs in town. So older, more experienced citizens wanted the jobs. Many of them had retail experience, and they knew how to manage employees. They could run their stores with fewer visits from district managers than younger American store managers. Second, New Zealand managers ordered baked goods from local bakeries. The food arrived fresh.

Back in the United States, Smith gathered his management team. They thought they could follow New Zealand's lead. They could hire older, more experienced store managers in small towns. They learned that a newly invented flash-freezing process could solve the challenge of delivering freshly baked goods. Starbucks already had regional bakeries for its big-city stores. Those bakeries could ship flash-frozen food to small towns. When thawed, the food still tasted fresh.

Playing Your Way to the Top

Want to learn how to become a company president? The powerRBrands virtual career game on Facebook will teach you how.

The goal of the game is to work your way to the top. Players face challenges that real-life businesses experience. They test their business skills. They practice making decisions. The winner becomes company president. He or she travels the virtual world earning and spending lots of money. If not, well…game over.

Reckitt Benckiser (RB) developed the game. RB is an international company that sells such consumer goods as Mucinex medicine for cough and congestion, Clearasil skin care products, and French's brand mustard and other foods.

The game is based on CEO Bart Becht's philosophy of business decisions. He says, "Constructive conflict drives better ideas than sitting around a table coming up with a consensus opinion."

Opening new stores in small towns became possible—and profitable. By 2010, there were 16,858 stores worldwide, according to Starbucks' timeline.

The decision not to expand into small towns had seemed a good one. Experience, investigation, and analysis said so. There were too many obstacles, but Starbucks' CEO found a way to overcome the obstacles. With solutions in place, the management team made a different decision that worked.

WEIGHING RISK

Many business decisions require an evaluation of the risks associated with the possibilities. But if a business leader is too afraid of what might happen, he or she may lose an opportunity. The Blackstone Group faced such a decision.

The Blackstone Group is an international business that specializes in investments. The company was considering buying a manufacturing company. It seemed like a good investment, but further

Asbestos is a mineral thought to cause cancer. Most business leaders would not purchase a company that used it. But the Blackstone Group weighed the risks and bought one anyway.

investigation found that the manufacturing company used asbestos.

Asbestos is a mineral that was once widely used in building and home construction, as well as other industries. Some

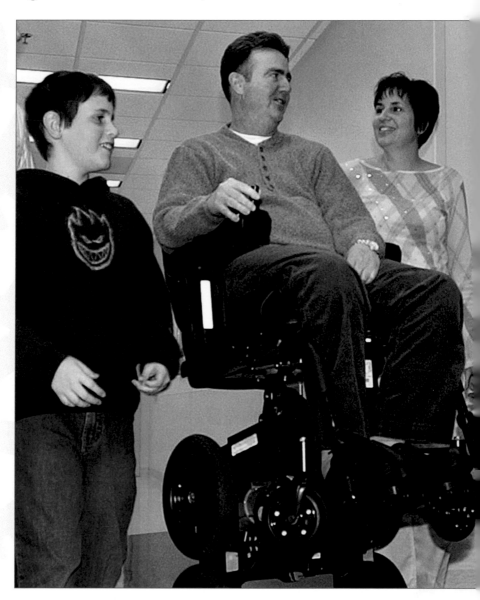

workers who inhaled asbestos particles came down with serious illnesses such as lung cancer and mesothelioma, cancer of the lining of the inside of the chest. Asbestos also posed another risk: lawsuits. Sick workers often filed lawsuits against their employers for exposing them to the material.

Blackstone's analysts feared that buying the manufacturer ran the risk of lawsuits, so they advised against the purchase.

However, Blackstone cofounder Steve Schwarzman saw an opportunity to make money. He wanted to learn more about the risk. He asked the analysts to get more information. They contacted engineers, lawyers, doctors, and insurance experts, as well as the manufacturing company itself. They found the risks of illness and lawsuits were low.

The company got its asbestos from another source. When the part arrived at the manufacturer, it was sealed in metal. The dangerous fibers could not escape into the air. The manufacturer's employees would not come in contact with it. Even if a problem occurred,

Teams of engineers competed to help management choose the best design for the iBOT wheelchair. The iBOT climbs stairs, rolls over curbs, and can rise to the eye level of people who are standing.

63

insurance would cover it. Blackstone decided to buy the manufacturing company, and the investment made a nice profit.

Which Design Is Best?

What if a business leader has doubts about an earlier decision? That was the situation Dean Kamen faced. Kamen is the founder and CEO of DEKA Research & Development Corporation. DEKA had joined with Johnson & Johnson to develop the iBOT. The iBOT is the world's most advanced wheelchair.

The iBOT imitates human balance. Users can rise to the eye level of someone who is standing. They can also climb stairs and ride over curbs.

DEKA had invested time and millions of dollars to develop a prototype of a design. A prototype is an example of the product before the product goes into mass production. Johnson & Johnson had already approved the design. Employees working on it thought the design was ready to go.

However, Kamen wanted to be sure the wheelchair was the best it could possibly be. During the design process, engineers had tried using two four-wheel clusters—one set on each side of the chair. There were other teams working on a design with three-wheel clusters and one with two-wheel clusters. The four-wheel design soon proved to be a bad idea. The team stopped working on it. The three-wheel design had few problems. It quickly reached a final form.

However, the two-wheel cluster had more promise. The seat could be lower. A user could pick up objects from the floor. The lower seat was also the right height for rolling up to a dining table. But the two-wheel version needed better controls, stronger materials, and a bigger motor. The team working on the two-wheel cluster version thought they could overcome the obstacles with more time. Kamen's employees agreed that the two-wheel version would be better if they could solve the problems. But not everyone believed they could. The three-wheel cluster version already worked.

After listening to both teams, Kamen decided to give the two-wheel team one more month. The engineers needed a little more time than that to finalize the design. But in the end, they convinced Kamen that they could make it work. And they did.

Ten Great Questions
to Ask a Business Leader

1. What kind of business intelligence does your company use to gather and analyze information?

2. What is your attitude toward risk when making decisions?

3. How do you evaluate whether a decision was a good one?

4. How much do you rely on emotion when you make a decision?

5. What issues have you faced working in a global economy?

6. Can you give me an example of a tactical decision that someone in your business made?

7. What cultural differences have affected decisions that your company leaders have made?

8. What have you learned from a bad business decision?

9. How can self-interest interfere with a good decision?

10. Why should decision makers be aware of close attachments to persons, places, or things?

GLOSSARY

accounting The function of keeping track of the financial activities of a business.

analyst A businessperson who separates an idea into its parts in order to learn about the idea as a whole.

bailout A loan for money to keep a company from going out of business.

business intelligence (BI) The technology used to collect, store, and interpret information that aids in the decision-making process; also called a decision support system.

chief executive officer (CEO) The top boss of a company. He or she is responsible for the day-to-day operations and reports to the board of directors.

class-action lawsuit A lawsuit in which a group of people with similar cases file a lawsuit together. The U.S. Supreme Court outlawed class-action suits in 2011.

consensus General agreement; an agreement that is "close enough" for group members to support.

exabyte One billion gigabytes.

knee-jerk reaction A quick decision based on emotion.

operations The day-to-day activities of a business in support of tactics and strategy.

profit The amount of money a company has left after subtracting the costs of doing business.

prototype An early model of a product created as an example before the product is widely manufactured.

real time A computer function that is happening "live."

recall An action by a product's manufacturer that asks people who bought the product to return it for repair.

strategy The overall plan for a business; the direction a company will follow for the long-term.

strike A situation in which employees stop work in order to protest such complaints as low pay or bad working conditions.

tactics The specific plans a company uses to carry out a strategy.

FOR MORE INFORMATION

Association of Information Technology Professionals
401 North Michigan Avenue, Suite 2400
Chicago, IL 60611-4267
(800) 224-9371
Web site: http://www.aitp.org
The Association of Information Technology Professionals
provides opportunities for employers, employees,
managers, programmers, students, and others to make
contacts and become more marketable in rapidly
changing technological careers.

Certified General Accountants Association of Canada
Suite 100, 4200 North Fraser Way
Burnaby, BC V5J 5K7
Canada
Web site: http://www.cga.org/canada
(604) 669-3555
The Certified General Accountants Association of Canada
represents certified general accountants and students in
Canada, Bermuda, the nations of the Caribbean, the
People's Republic of China, and Hong Kong. The
association sets educational and professional standards
and advocates for professional excellence.

Council for Economic Education
122 East 42nd Street, Suite 2600
New York, NY 10168
(800) 338-1192
Web site: http://www.councilforeconed.org
The Council for Economic Education advocates for better
    school-based economic and personal finance education.
    It offers educational programs and teacher resources.

Decision Education Foundation
745 Emerson Street
Palo Alto, CA 94301-2411
(650) 475-4474
Web site: http://www.decisioneducation.org
The Decision Education Foundation is an association of
    educators, decision scientists, and successful
    businesspeople who seek to teach young people the basic
    skills they'll need to make decisions.

Information Technology Association of Canada
5090 Explorer Drive, Suite 801
Mississauga, ON L4W 4T9
Canada
(905) 602-8345
Web site: http://www.itac.ca
The Information Technology Association of Canada
    represents a diverse group of people who work with the
    strategic use of technology in such areas as
    telecommunications, Internet services, hardware,
    microelectronics, software, and electronic content.

JA Worldwide
One Education Way
Colorado Springs, CO 80906
(719) 540-8000
Web site: http://www.ja.org
JA Worldwide's purpose is to inspire and prepare young
people to succeed in a global economy. Junior
Achievement programs teach students about
employment readiness, business, and finance to prepare
them for the real world.

National Association of Corporate Directors
Two Lafayette Centre
1133 21st Street NW, Suite 700
Washington, DC 20036
(202) 775-0509
Web site: http://www.nacdonline.org
The National Association of Corporate Directors provides
information to members of boards of directors of public,
private, family, nonprofit, and cooperative companies
from a variety of industries. It provides information and
insights to help members perform effectively and
efficiently.

Society for Judgment and Decision Making
College of Business
P.O. Box 3061110
Florida State University
Tallahassee, FL 32306-1110
Web site: http://www.sjdm.org

The Society for Judgment and Decision Making is an academic organization for the study of theories of judgments and decisions. Its members include psychologists, economists, organizational researchers, decision analysts, and other decision researchers. It also publishes the journal *Judgment and Decision Making*.

WEB SITES

Due to the changing nature of Internet links, Rosen Publishing has developed an online list of Web sites related to the subject of this book. This site is updated regularly. Please use this link to access the list:

http://www.rosenlinks.com/rwe/bizde

FOR FURTHER READING

Bell, Robert. *From Lifeguard to Sun King: The Man Behind the Banana Boat Success Story*. El Monte, CA: W Business Books, 2008.

Bodden, Valerie. *The Story of Coca-Cola*. Mankato, MN: Creative Paperbacks, 2011.

Bodden, Valerie. *The Story of Disney*. Mankato, MN: Creative Paperbacks, 2011.

Cathy, S. Truett. *How Did You Do It, Truett?* Aurora, ON, Canada: Looking Glass Press, 2007.

Covey, Sean. *The 6 Most Important Decisions You'll Ever Make: A Guide for Teens*. New York, NY: Fireside, 2006.

Frisch, Aaron. *Built for Success: The Story of Nike*. Mankato, MN: Creative Paperbacks, 2011.

Gilbert, Sara. *The Story of Google*. Mankato, MN: Creative Paperbacks, 2011.

Gilbert, Sara. *The Story of McDonald's*. Mankato, MN: Creative Paperbacks, 2011.

Musolf, Nell. *The Story of Microsoft*. Mankato, MN: Creative Paperbacks, 2011.

Scheps, Swain. *Business Intelligence for Dummies*. Indianapolis, IN: Wiley, 2008.

Watanabe, Ken. *Problem Solving 101*. New York, NY: Penguin Group, 2009.

BIBLIOGRAPHY

Anderson, Curt, and Greg Bluestein. "Class-Action Suits
    May Cost Toyota Billions." Associated Press/MSNBC.
    com, March 9, 2010. Retrieved February 24, 2011
    (http://www.msnbc.msn.com/id/35776697/ns/
    business-autos/#).

Articlesbase.com. "Decision Making in Business." February
    16, 2009. Retrieved January 15, 2011 (http://www.
    articlesbase.com/business-articles/decision-making-in-
    business-773367.html).

Bannister, Steve. "The Secrets of Effective Decision-Making."
    CanadaOne, November 2006. Retrieved January 15,
    2011 (http://www.canadaone.com/ezine/nov06/
    effective_decision_making.html).

Beach, Emily. "Facts About Nike Sweatshops." eHow.com.
    Retrieved February 4, 2011 (http://www.ehow.com/
    print/about_5485125_nike-sweatshops.html).

Bowett, Richard. "Organisation—Decision-Making in
    Business." Tutor2u. Retrieved January 14, 2011
    (http://tutor2u.net/business/organisation/
    decisionmaking.htm).

Brett, Jeanne, Kristin Behfar, and Mary C. Kern. "Managing
    Multicultural Teams." *Harvard Business Review*,
    November 2006, pp. 87–96.

Close-up Media. "Research and Markets Adds Report: The New Symbiosis of Professional Networks: Social Media's Impact on Business and Decision-Making." *Entertainment Close-up*, December 23, 2010.

Contact Communications. "RFID Enabled Real-Time Production Monitoring at Sewing Floor." *Stitch World*, April 1, 2010.

Dittmer, Robert E., and Stephanie McFarland. *151 Quick Ideas for Delegating and Decision Making*. Franklin Lakes, NJ: Career Press, 2007.

Finkelstein, Sydney, Jo Whitehead, and Andrew Campbell. *Think Again: Why Good Leaders Make Bad Decisions and How to Keep It from Happening to You*. Boston, MA: Harvard Business Publishing, 2008.

Harvard Business Review. The Essential Guide to Leadership. Boston, MA: Harvard Business School Publishing, 2009.

Harvard Business Review. On Making Smarter Decisions. Boston, MA: Harvard Business School Publishing, 2007.

Lavalle, Steve, and William Fuessler. "Reaching for Analytics." *Business Finance*, Vol. 15, No. 5, July–August 2009, pp. 34–38.

Ludvigsen, Karl. "Not So Sclerotic: The Truth About General Motors." *Spectator*, Vol. 311, No. 9459, December 12, 2009, pp. 30–31.

Luecke, Richard. *Decision Making: 5 Steps to Better Results*. Boston, MA: Harvard Business School Publishing, 2006.

Malpica, Richard. "Business Intelligence, the Smart Way." *Commercial Property News*, March 12, 2009.

March, James G. *A Primer on Decision Making: How Decisions Happen*. New York, NY: The Free Press, 2009.

McKendrick, Joe. "The Year Ahead in Information Management: Smarter, Cloudier, and Greener." *Database Trends and Applications*, Vol. 23, No. 4, December 2009, pp. 6–9.

National Defense University. "Strategic Leadership and Decision Making: Consensus Team Decision Making." Retrieved January 14, 2010 (http://www.au.af.mil/au/awc/awcgate/ndu/strat-ldr-dm/pt3ch11.html).

Olsen, Keith. "Business Decision Making Process." eHow.com. Retrieved January 15, 2011 (http://www.ehow.com/how-does_5166708_business-decision-making-process.html).

PBS NewsHour Science Reports. "Military Expanding Role of Robots on the Battlefield." Transcript. Original air date April 23, 2009.

Raman, Rakesh. "The Tech Soothsayer." *Dataquest*, August 6, 2010.

Reed Business Information. "Business Analytics in Decision-making." *Computer Weekly*, September 21, 2010.

United Business Media. "Data on Demand from P&G's 'Cockpit.'" *Information Week*, September 13, 2010, p. 72.

Walsh, Dustin. "No Secrets: Businesses Find It Pays to Open Books to Employees." *Crain's Detroit Business*, Vol. 26, No. 3, January 18, 2010, p. 11.

Zeckhauser, Bryn, and Aaron Sandoski. *How the Wise Decide: The Lessons of 21 Extraordinary Leaders*. New York, NY: Crown Business, 2008.

Ziff Davis Enterprise. "Business Analytics Numbers and Nuance." *CIO Insight*, January 12, 2011.

INDEX

G

General Motors, 52–54
goals, defining, 7–9
good decisions, elements of,
        12–14
Google, 14
Granger, John, 14, 34, 47
gut reactions/feelings, 14

H

Hayashi, Alden M., 11
Hertz, 39

I

IBM Summit at Start, 34
iBOT, 64
information technology (IT),
        32–34
intuition/instinct, 5, 11, 14

J

Johnson & Johnson, 64

K

Kamen, Dean, 64–65
Kansas City Voices, 25
knee-jerk reactions, 27–29

L

LinkedIn, 42, 44

M

MAARS, 23
majority rule, as way of making
        decision, 29–30
Meltzer, Brad, 44

N

natural ability, 12–14
Nike, 45–47, 52

O

open-book management, 29
open mind, keeping an, 12
operational decisions, 22, 23

P

Plato, 11
powerRBrands, 59
profit, explanation of, 7
pros and cons, weighing of as way
        of making decision, 10, 31

R

real-time, explanation of, 32
Reckitt Benckiser (RB), 59
risk, 10, 19, 20, 32, 48, 60
robots, battlefield, 23

S

Schwarzman, Steve, 63
Sealed Air, 4–5, 19

About the Author

Mary-Lane Kamberg makes business decisions every day. She is a professional writer and author of nonfiction books for children and teens.

Photo Credits

Cover (handshake), p 1. (lower right) © www.istockphoto.com/Chagin; cover (headline) © www.istockphoto.com/Lilli Day; pp. 6, 8–9, 24, 50 Shutterstock.com; pp. 7, 18, 27, 36, 45, 55 ghosted photo by Mario Tama/Getty Images; p. 13 Keith Brofsky/Photodisc/Thinkstock; p. 15 Sean Gallup/Getty Images; pp. 20–21 Chris Clinton/Digital Vision/Thinkstock; p. 22 Fuse/Getty Images; p. 28 Jon Feingersh/Blend Images/Getty Images; p. 30 © Jeff Greenberg/The Image Works; p. 33 H. Armstrong Roberts/Retrofile/Getty Images; pp. 37, 53 Bloomberg via Getty Images; p. 40 Ryouchin/Digital Vision/Getty Images; p. 43 Frederick M. Brown/Getty Images; p. 46 AFP/Getty Images; pp. 56–57 Frederic J. Brown/AFP/Getty Images; pp. 60–61 Astrid & Hanns-Frieder Michler/Photo Researchers, Inc.; pp. 62–63 © AP Images; cover and interior graphic elements: © www.istockphoto.com/Andrey Prokhorov (front cover), © www.istockphoto.com/Dean Turner (back cover and interior pages), © www.istockphoto.com/Darja Tokranova (p. 17); © www.istockphoto.com/articular (p. 66); © www.istockphoto.com/studiovision (pp. 67, 69, 73, 74, 77); © www.istockphoto.com/Chen Fu Soh (multiple interior pages).

Designer: Nicole Russo; Editor: Bethany Bryan;
Photo Researcher: Marty Levick